INS-CREATIONS
(INSPIRED CREATIONS)

INS-CREATIONS
(INSPIRED CREATIONS)

RENETTE CANTY, MPH, MBA, CIT

HOV
PUBLISHING

Ins-Creations
(Inspired Creations)

All Scripture quotations, unless otherwise indicated, are taken from the King James version of The Holy Bible.

HOV Publishing is a division of HOV, LLC.
email: hopeofvision@gmail.com
www.hovpub.com

Front Cover Design by
Inside layout by HOV Design Solutions
Editing: HOV Publishing Editing Team

ISBN Paperback: 978-1-955107-20-4
ISBN eBook: 978-1-955107-19-8

Printed in the United States of America

DEDICATION

Firstly, I am ever grateful to my Lord and Savior, Jesus Christ. It is because of His continued grace and mercies in my life that I can continue. I thank Him for every mountain He has enabled me to climb and every valley He has brought me through.

This book is dedicated to the memory of my precious mother, whom I've only known through the reminiscent thoughts of those who told me about her before she departed this earth at a very young age. Additionally, I dedicate this book to my dear sisters (and brothers-in-law): Paula (Grady), Pamela (Rick), and Annette (Kelvin), for their constant love and encouragement. I also dedicate this book to my dear friend Jennifer, who is one of my biggest supporters in everything

I do. My nephew, Jonathan, I love you. I dedicate this book to the memory of my former pastor and mentor, Bishop Iona E. Locke, who encouraged me to look inside myself and see the "wealth" God has put there. I dedicate this book to my cousin, Dr. Michelle Wells, who took time to hear me and put me in touch with the right resources to get it done. Lastly, I dedicate this work to my spiritual leaders, District Elder Kameron L. Adams and First Lady Jordan Adams, who have committed their lives to serving God's people unconditionally.

CONTENTS

PREFACE   ix

ONE   **KEEP STRIVING**   1

TWO   **YEA THOUGH I WALK**   5

THREE   **EMMANUEL (God with Us)**   11

FOUR   **LET ME TELL YOU**   15

FIVE   **A TRUE FRIEND**   19

SIX   **OUR FAMILY**   25

SEVEN   **THIS FAR BY FAITH**   31

EIGHT   **HAVE FAITH IN JESUS**   35

NINE   **ANCHORED**   39

TEN   **WASHED IN JESUS' BLOOD**   43

ELEVEN   **WE ARE MISSIONARIES**   47

TWELVE   **A PRAYER**   51

THIRTEEN **GRATITUDES**   55

FOURTEEN **OF SUCH IS THE KINGDOM OF HEAVEN** 59

FIFTEEN **PRAISE** — 63

SIXTEEN **THE RAPTURE** — 69

SEVENTEEN **STRIVING TO BE** — 75

EIGHTEEN **ALL THINGS** — 79

NINETEEN **MANY SAINTS OF TODAY** — 83

TWENTY **TO JESUS** — 89

TWENTY-ONE **ANOTHER YEAR** — 93

TWENTY-TWO **THE LORD'S GOODNESS** — 97

TWENTY-THREE **STAND UP FOR JESUS** — 101

TWENTY-FOUR **SINCE I MET JESUS** — 105

TWENTY-FIVE **HOLY MASTER** — 109

ABOUT THE AUTHOR — 113

PREFACE

I began this work not with the end in mind, but with the aspiration of encouraging someone to look deep inside themselves and pull out the creativity that God has deposited within them from birth, using it to the best of their abilities to encourage others. Life is an ongoing process in which each of us plays a special part in enhancing our own lives and those of others through song, dance, poetry, drama, kindness, love, a smile, hope, understanding, or whatever talents we have been endowed with. This book of poetry and short writings was inspired through the auspices of the Holy Ghost many years ago. In fact, I wrote the first poem in 1981. After writing several more over the course of several years, I put them in a binder and set them on a shelf–until now.

The purpose of this book is to share the sentiments of my heart through different phases of my life in hopes of inspiring you not to give up, but to keep striving to accomplish your goals. As a Christian, I have found that God is my everything, including the best friend I could ever have. He inspired me to write instead of giving up when things got tough, and I hope you will be inspired by these writings too. This book did not happen overnight; it came to fruition when I regained my focus and refused to allow life to get the best of me. I always kept the words of these poems in the back of my mind and vowed to share them with the world one day.

Several years ago, one of my former pastors told me, "Renette, your wealth is inside you." I thought about it over and over and eventually filed it away in the back of my mind. Even so, I could never forget those words and wondered what my pastor could have been talking about. After praying to God for understanding, He reminded me about the wealth of poetry and words of wisdom that He had given me over the years. Thus, this anthology is to comfort and encourage people who may feel helpless, friendless, forgotten, and alone. The gifts that God has placed inside me do not have a monetary price; they are priceless. Therefore, it is my job to use every gift and talent for His glory. Be blessed.

Renette Canty

INS-CREATIONS
(INSPIRED CREATIONS)

POEM
ONE
KEEP STRIVING

Sometimes the easiest thing to do in the face of adversity is to give up, walk away, and pretend it didn't happen. But that won't help us get rid of the nagging feeling in the back of our minds about what we could have accomplished if we had been more patient. Keep striving!

KEEP STRIVING
April 5, 1981

Keep striving, the Lord has a great work
for you to do.
He is your only source of strength;
He will see you through.
Your mountains will get higher,
and your valleys will deepen, but forever press
toward the high calling mark and your reward
will be great in the end.

Many battles you have fought and many more
will come, but since you have the Lord on your
side, you can count them already won!

The enemy is very busy trying to destroy
whomever he will, but the Lord has promised to
fight our battles if only we keep still!

Therefore, keep the Lord as your shepherd,
Let Him guide you day by day.
Stand steadfast in righteousness and He will
strengthen you along the way.

INS-CREATIONS NOTES:

_____

_____

_____

_____

_____

_____

_____

_____

_____

_____

_____

_____

_____

_____

_____

_____

_____

_____

_____

_____

_____

_____

INS-CREATIONS NOTES:

POEM
TWO

YEA THOUGH I WALK

Oh, to be alive and well with everything going the way we want them to all the time is unrealistic and oftentimes more so true for many people than it is for others. Even so, whenever we must face difficulties and take life journeys through unknown territories, stay encouraged and focused. As Christians, we are never alone because God is always with us. Therefore, we should always trust Him to lead us through whatever circumstances that seem too difficult for us to handle and keep walking forward.

YEA THOUGH I WALK
1984

As I walk the path of righteousness,
I will never fear.
I will keep a heart of faithfulness because
Jesus is always near.

Though Satan jumps and mocks
as if he is going to attack,
This gives me no cause to stop.
I won't ever look back.

The Lord is my shepherd,
all I must do is trust Him.
I will follow in His footsteps and never
let my light grow dim.

Yea though I walk,

I will count all life's unpleasantries

as nothing compared

To the promise of eternal life when

the victory is won!

INS-CREATIONS NOTES:

_____

_____

_____

_____

_____

_____

_____

_____

_____

_____

_____

_____

_____

_____

_____

_____

_____

_____

_____

INS-CREATIONS NOTES:

_____
_____
_____
_____
_____
_____
_____
_____
_____
_____
_____
_____
_____
_____
_____
_____
_____
_____

INS-CREATIONS NOTES:

_____

_____

_____

_____

_____

_____

_____

_____

_____

_____

_____

_____

_____

_____

_____

_____

_____

_____

_____

_____

POEM
THREE

EMMANUEL (God with Us)

Jesus promised never to leave us or turn His
back on us, and it is true. I know that there are
times when it seems like we are alone because I
have felt like that too. Don't be fooled; you are
never alone if you have Christ in your life.
Although we will acquire friends throughout our
lives, there are times when they cannot be with
us. Just know that Emmanuel is always with you;
just trust Him.

EMMANUEL (God with Us)

Thank God for the good times and
the bad times too.
Thank Him for the many smiles and tears
He has brought us through.

No, we are not walking alone,
and we must keep looking up.
We allow our hearts to sing a happy song
because God is always with us.

I thank God for the victory and
many people I will tell.
I will run this race with patience and shout,
Emmanuel!!

INS-CREATIONS NOTES:

_____

_____

_____

_____

_____

_____

_____

_____

_____

_____

_____

_____

_____

_____

_____

_____

_____

_____

_____

_____

INS-CREATIONS NOTES:

_____

_____

_____

_____

_____

_____

_____

_____

_____

_____

_____

_____

_____

_____

_____

_____

_____

_____

_____

_____

POEM
FOUR

LET ME TELL YOU

Have you ever had something to tell your family or friends that you thought was the greatest news? You were nearly bursting with excitement as you waited for the opportunity to get to them so that you could share the good news. I am sure that we all have had moments like that, and we can smile as we think back on moments like those because they have created such wonderful memories for us. Well, I have news to share with you now, let me tell you.

LET ME TELL YOU
1983

Let me tell you about my friend!

Oh, He is my joy divine!

He is the greatest and strongest of all men,

He just has my mind.

I was considered unworthy,

but my friend loved me anyway,

Enough to shed His precious blood;

Oh, what a price to pay!

My friend did it for me and I gave Him my soul.

From sin I am now freed because my friend

made me whole.

I love my friend and He is the best one

that I have.

My friend's name is Jesus.

Do you know Him?

INS-CREATIONS NOTES:

_____

_____

_____

_____

_____

_____

_____

_____

_____

_____

_____

_____

_____

_____

_____

_____

_____

_____

_____

_____

INS-CREATIONS NOTES:

_____

_____

_____

_____

_____

_____

_____

_____

_____

_____

_____

_____

_____

_____

_____

_____

_____

_____

_____

_____

_____

_____

POEM
FIVE

TRUE FRIEND

Sometimes you just need someone to talk to, to share with; someone to simply listen to you and hear the sentiments of your heart. However, you don't want to share with anybody who does not value and respect you. That is why you need a true friend. Someone who loves you unconditionally and without judgement.

TRUE FRIEND
1984

What is a friend, one may ask? Is he easy to find?
What characteristics does he have? Are they
compatible with mine?
I don't know what others will say, but I'll tell you
about the One I know.

We walk and talk together every day.
Oh, how I love Him so!
His personality is so warm.
He is friendly and very kind.

Oh, I wouldn't take all the world for this
precious friend of mine!
One day I was in trouble. I was sinking in despair,
But my friend looked at me lovingly and gave His
life to get me out of there.

My friend lives in Heaven.

Oh, but He is ever so close,

Because He also lives in my heart

as the precious Holy Ghost.

I don't worry about him leaving me

and going away with another,

Because Jesus Christ is a friend

that stays closer than any brother!

INS-CREATIONS NOTES:

INS-CREATIONS NOTES:

_____

_____

_____

_____

_____

_____

_____

_____

_____

_____

_____

_____

_____

_____

_____

_____

_____

_____

_____

INS-CREATIONS NOTES:

_____

_____

_____

_____

_____

_____

_____

_____

_____

_____

_____

_____

_____

_____

_____

_____

_____

_____

_____

_____

_____

_____

POEM
SIX

OUR FAMILY

I don't know about you, but I love my family. It is made up of my sisters, brother, brother in laws, nephews, nieces, cousins, my maternal aunt, maternal uncle, close friends, my precious pets, and of course, I will never forget my parents and grandparents. What is a family? A family is a friend that is always willing to lend a hand. A family is an organization of love and support. Even as Christians, we are a family that represents the vast and precious body of Christ.

OUR FAMILY

1981

We represent a family greater than
any other on earth.
One that is far more valuable than rubies
and all money is worth.

We are blessed above all others
and our Father is a king.
He said that if we ask and believe
we shall not lack anything.

He showers us with his grace and
strengthens us with His love.
He filled us with His spirit and
made us all as one.

We represent a family unlike any other one around; we are of every race and color. We represent the family of God.

INS-CREATIONS NOTES:

INS-CREATIONS NOTES:

_____

_____

_____

_____

_____

_____

_____

_____

_____

_____

_____

_____

_____

_____

_____

_____

_____

_____

_____

_____

INS-CREATIONS NOTES:

Poem
SEVEN

THIS FAR BY FAITH

If you haven't heard, and I am sure that you have, the entire world has been impacted by so many traumatic events in the last few years. Many people who were here a few years ago are not hear because of the results of the pandemic and other weapons of mass destruction, some of which occurred at the hands of individuals who were determined to carry out the plans of evil hidden in their hearts. Even so, I am here by the grace of God, I am thankful and I am determined to walk by faith. For we walk by faith, not by sight. (2 Corinthians 5:7)

THIS FAR BY FAITH
1985

I have come this far by faith,

not by any works that I have done.

I keep trusting in God's good grace and His

mercies new every morn.

Tests and trials have come to me, but my

victories outweighed them all.

God's love keeps holding my feet,

keeping me from a terrible fall.

Each day is a new beginning to give

God my very best,

Because in Him I have my being

as I strive for that perfect rest.

There is no better way than

to live my life for Him.

He brought me this far by faith

and I know He will do it again!

INS-CREATIONS NOTES:

_____

_____

_____

_____

_____

_____

_____

_____

_____

_____

_____

_____

_____

_____

_____

_____

_____

_____

_____

INS-CREATIONS NOTES:

POEM
EIGHT

HAVE FAITH IN JESUS

Let me encourage you to put your trust in Jesus
and keep it there. Do not vacillate regardless of
your circumstances in life. Don't trust him one
day and doubt the next. Trust Him all the time
because He will never leave you. Jesus knows
what is best for you, and He also knows what is
best for me. "Trust in the Lord with all thine
heart; and lean not unto thine own
understanding," (Proverbs 3:5)

HAVE FAITH IN JESUS
1988

Cast thy burdens upon the Lord

and have faith in Him.

He is a very present help in trouble,

He is our strength.

We will never understand all His ways,

but He is the all-wise one.

He provides for us every day and

for that alone we give Him honor.

So, wherever we must sojourn through

the shadows of this land,

We will put our hands in Jesus' hands

and keep the faith in Him.

INS-CREATIONS NOTES:

_____

_____

_____

_____

_____

_____

_____

_____

_____

_____

_____

_____

_____

_____

_____

_____

_____

_____

_____

INS-CREATIONS NOTES:

_____

_____

_____

_____

_____

_____

_____

_____

_____

_____

_____

_____

_____

_____

_____

_____

_____

_____

_____

_____

_____

POEM
NINE

ANCHORED

There have been many times in my life where I made decisions but changed my mind. I decided to do something different from my original plans because I thought it was for the best and most suitable for my needs or what I wanted to accomplish at the time. Changing my mind about living for Jesus is not an option for me currently nor any other time. Jesus is the very reason for my existence, and if it had not been for him, I would not have an opportunity for eternal life.

ANCHORED

1986

Like a tree planted by the rivers of water,
may my soul forever be,

That no leaf should wither but always
abide in prosperity.

The storms of life are raging, but my
foundation is steadfast and sure

Because my soul is anchored in Jesus
by the magnificence of His power.

I am determined to run this race because
I must redeem the time, and as I work toward my
heavenly home, I will show the way to mankind.

I will meditate in God's word with a heart to
endure so that my soul remains anchored,

standing steadfast and sure.

INS-CREATIONS NOTES:

_____

_____

_____

_____

_____

_____

_____

_____

_____

_____

_____

_____

_____

_____

_____

_____

_____

_____

_____

_____

INS-CREATIONS NOTES:

_____

_____

_____

_____

_____

_____

_____

_____

_____

_____

_____

_____

_____

_____

_____

_____

_____

_____

_____

_____

_____

POEM
TEN

WASHED IN JESUS' BLOOD

Many people pay more attention to what they look like on the outside than what they look like on the inside. No doubt, it is important to take care of our health, keep ourselves groomed, and always do our best to look our best. However, there is another side to us that we need to focus on as well. We must be especially careful to keep our hearts, minds, and souls clean, which can only be accomplished through the blood of Jesus Christ. According to 1 John 1:6-7, "If we say that we have fellowship with him, and walk in darkness, we lie, and do not the truth: But if we walk in the light, as he is in the light, we have fellowship one with another, and the blood of Jesus Christ his Son cleanseth us from all sin.

"WASHED IN JESUS' BLOOD
1979

I have been washed in the blood of Jesus
and cleansed from all my sins.
I am filled with the Holy Spirit; my soul
has new life therein.
My weak soul has been strengthened,
I feel happy and brand new.
I have been washed in the blood of Jesus;
I have been born anew.
My life is dedicated to the Lord,
I am living to do His will.
I know that He will fight all my battles
if I will trust Him still.
I have been washed in the blood of Jesus;
I thank Him again and again.
I have been washed in the blood of Jesus;
He is my Savior and friend!

INS-CREATIONS NOTES:

_____

_____

_____

_____

_____

_____

_____

_____

_____

_____

_____

_____

_____

_____

_____

_____

_____

_____

_____

INS-CREATIONS NOTES:

_____

_____

_____

_____

_____

_____

_____

_____

_____

_____

_____

_____

_____

_____

_____

_____

_____

_____

_____

_____

_____

_____

POEM
ELEVEN

WE ARE MISSIONARIES

Have you ever wondered why you were born? Everybody has a specific purpose, planned by God to be on this earth. As Christians, we are chosen to be a light to those who are in darkness in this strange land called Earth. Therefore, we are like missionaries sent on a mission to help bring others into the faith. The people we help may be our family, friends, co-workers, or people in the communities we live in. The important thing for us to do is to reach out to someone with a kind word or gesture whenever we can.

WE ARE MISSIONARIES

1985

We are missionaries; like a city set up on a hill.

We are on a great journey to do the Master's will.

Our candles are burning bright
for all the world to see,

That the way into the light is through Jesus, only!

Whatever our hands find to do
we must do it with cheer,

Working before the day is through because
night is almost here.

INS-CREATIONS NOTES:

_____

_____

_____

_____

_____

_____

_____

_____

_____

_____

_____

_____

_____

_____

_____

_____

_____

_____

_____

_____

INS-CREATIONS NOTES:

POEM
TWELVE

A PRAYER

Sometimes in life, there will be times when we
don't have words to express our gratitude to
Jesus for all that he has done for us. That is
alright, and a sincere prayer to him will always be
in order. I am sure that just as we like to be told
"thank you" for what we do for others, Jesus also
appreciates expressions of gratitude from us
sometimes too. Don't forget, tell him thank you
every day; you will be glad that you did.

A PRAYER
1984

Jesus, I thank You for loving everyone.

For loving us unconditionally,

and in truth; proven by Your birth.

You came from heaven to earth

in the form of human flesh,

was laid in a lowly manger,

and the news quickly spread.

You came with a purpose;

nothing could change Your mind.

You came to save the lost,

sin-sick souls of all mankind.

Yes, Jesus, I thank You for all that

You have done.

I sincerely thank You for loving everyone.

INS-CREATIONS NOTES:

_____
_____
_____
_____
_____
_____
_____
_____
_____
_____
_____
_____
_____
_____
_____
_____
_____
_____
_____
_____

INS-CREATIONS NOTES:

_____

_____

_____

_____

_____

_____

_____

_____

_____

_____

_____

_____

_____

_____

_____

_____

_____

_____

_____

_____

_____

_____

POEM
THIRTEEN

GRATITUDE

The Bible reminds us to be thankful to God <u>in</u> all things because it is His will, (I Thessalonians 5:18). Many people misinterpret that to mean that we are to give thanks for everything, but that is incorrect. Although we will experience many disappointments in life, as Christians, we should always give God thanks while we are going through the situations. He is worthy of all our praises through the good times as well as the not-so-good times.

GRATITUDE
1982

Be thankful for the age you lived to be and
count it an honor from the Lord.

Be grateful for the birthdays you have lived to
see and count them an honor from the Lord.

Many people who were born when you were,
have gone on into eternity.

They had hopes and plans for their lives,
but now their dreams will never be.

Thankfully live this new year of your life
in deed and in word, and count it nothing less
than an honor from the Lord.

INS-CREATIONS NOTES:

_____

_____

_____

_____

_____

_____

_____

_____

_____

_____

_____

_____

_____

_____

_____

_____

_____

_____

_____

_____

_____

INS-CREATIONS NOTES:

_____

_____

_____

_____

_____

_____

_____

_____

_____

_____

_____

_____

_____

_____

_____

_____

_____

_____

_____

_____

Poem
FOURTEEN

OF SUCH IS THE KINGDOM OF HEAVEN

In the King James version of the Bible, the Gospel according to Matthew, chapter 19, verse 14, it says, "But Jesus said, suffer little children, and forbid them not, to come unto me: for of such is the kingdom of heaven." There is nothing so pure and innocent as the love and trust that little children have in their parents. They look to their mother and father to take care of them, to teach and nurture them, to show them the differences between right and wrong, and to protect them. That is the kind of faith that Jesus looks for in all Chrisian believers; the faith that is childlike.

OF SUCH IS THE KINGDOM OF HEAVEN

1980

Jesus loves all children no matter what
their na-tion-a-lity!

He made them all great examples for
the whole wide world to see.

He has a plan established for the salvation
of all mankind,

And his children have the secret;
please keep this in mind.

If you want to enter God's kingdom, you must be
humble as a child.

Put all your trust in him and wait patiently
all the while.

So, even as a child of God, I truly wish to say,

I want to be an example of Christ with every
passing day!

INS-CREATIONS NOTES:

_____

_____

_____

_____

_____

_____

_____

_____

_____

_____

_____

_____

_____

_____

_____

_____

_____

_____

_____

INS-CREATIONS NOTES:

_____

_____

_____

_____

_____

_____

_____

_____

_____

_____

_____

_____

_____

_____

_____

_____

_____

_____

_____

POEM
FIFTEEN

PRAISE

The Holy Scriptures instruct us to give thanks
in everything because it is God's will
(1 Thessalonians 5:18) concerning His children.
However, some people may wonder why God
would want us to give thanks when we are sick,
hurt, or going through a tough time. But
remember, we are not truly exercising our faith
in God, nor our true love for Him, until we praise
and give Him thanks while we are facing
difficulties. Of course, it is easy to praise God
when all is going well, but we have a
responsibility to praise Him all the time.

PRAISE

1983

Yes, Lord, I started this journey
depending on You, hoping and trusting
that You would see me through.

Hallelujah, hallelujah, see me through!

I have witnessed so much joy that can't
all be told about how Your spirit has
moved down in my soul.

Hallelujah, hallelujah, in my soul!

I have experienced many heartaches,
sicknesses, tests, and trials,
But I thank You, Lord,
for being with me each mile.

Hallelujah, hallelujah, with me each mile.

I thank You, Lord, for being my best friend,
And for proving it again and again.

Hallelujah, hallelujah, proving it again and again!

You brought me this far and I will
keep walking with You
Because I know, dear Lord, that You
will see me through.

Hallelujah, hallelujah, see me through.

INS-CREATIONS NOTES:

INS-CREATIONS NOTES:

_____
_____
_____
_____
_____
_____
_____
_____
_____
_____
_____
_____
_____
_____
_____
_____
_____
_____
_____
_____
_____

INS-CREATIONS NOTES:

Poem
SIXTEEN

THE RAPTURE

For the Lord Himself shall descend from heaven with a shout, with the voice of the archangel, and with the trumpet of God: and the dead in Christ shall rise first. Then we who are alive and remain shall be caught up together with them in the clouds, to meet the Lord in the air: and so shall we ever be with the Lord.

(1 Thessalonians 4:16-17)

THE RAPURE

1979

I don't know when Jesus will come, but take a

look in the Bible at Matthew 24:41.

It says that two were grinding there

right at the mill;

One was taken and the other was left here.

The one that was taken was a child of God, the

one left evidently was not.

We better turn from evil ways, and let's get right.

Jesus Christ is coming like a thief in the night.

(1 Thessalonians 5:2)

If you don't believe what I'm telling you, take a

look in the Bible at Matthew 25:2.

It's talking about the wise and the foolish; they

were then as we are today.

The wise are the ones that will have eternal life.

The foolish are the ones that will not

reign with Christ.

We better repent of our sins and be born again.

When the door is closed no one can get in.

Written by

Annette and Renette Canty

INS-CREATIONS NOTES:

_____

_____

_____

_____

_____

_____

_____

_____

_____

_____

_____

_____

_____

_____

_____

_____

_____

_____

_____

_____

_____

_____

INS-CREATIONS NOTES:

_____

_____

_____

_____

_____

_____

_____

_____

_____

_____

_____

_____

_____

_____

_____

_____

_____

_____

_____

INS-CREATIONS NOTES:

_____

_____

_____

_____

_____

_____

_____

_____

_____

_____

_____

_____

_____

_____

_____

_____

_____

_____

_____

_____

_____

POEM
SEVENTEEN

STRIVING TO BE

Is there something greater that you want to do with your life? Have you made efforts to achieve your goals but stopped because you ran into opposition? Let me encourage you by telling you not to give up on your dreams. Anything worth having requires what my grandmother use to call "elbow grease." In other words, you must put a lot of time, effort, and patience into bringing your goals into fruition. Importantly, as Christians, the word of God tells us in Psalm 37:4 that if you delight yourself in the Lord, He will give you the desires of your heart. Do not ever give up.

STRIVING TO BE

1983

I am only one in the number, yet I must still
do my best, to please my heavenly father;
I have no time for rest.
Although Satan keeps trying to stop me,
I must never look behind, so that I can follow
wherever Jesus leads me and hear when he
speaks to my mind.
I never want to become slothful or sluggish
along my way, because Jesus is always faithful,
and I want to give him my best every day.
Therefore, I must watch and pray,
and always strive to be one of God's precious
saints, and a faithful missionary.

INS-CREATIONS NOTES:

_____

_____

_____

_____

_____

_____

_____

_____

_____

_____

_____

_____

_____

_____

_____

_____

_____

_____

_____

_____

INS-CREATIONS NOTES:

_____

_____

_____

_____

_____

_____

_____

_____

_____

_____

_____

_____

_____

_____

_____

_____

_____

_____

_____

_____

POEM
EIGHTEEN

ALL THINGS

Whenever you feel like you cannot continue and all hope is lost, always remember, you can go on! Philippians 4:13 encourages us with these words, "I can do all things through Christ which strengtheneth me." Remember, your strength comes from Jesus so stop trying to do everything by yourself.

ALL THINGS

1985

I can do all things through Christ who
strengthens me.

When my days get dark and dreary with
problems on every hand,

I don't ever have to worry because
Jesus will help me stand.

When Satan comes my way, temptations
he will bring, but my faith lies in Jesus Christ;
through Him, I can do all things.

I will keep standing steadfast, walking in the
liberty, no longer bound by this world because
Jesus has made me free.

INS-CREATIONS NOTES:

INS-CREATIONS NOTES:

_____

_____

_____

_____

_____

_____

_____

_____

_____

_____

_____

_____

_____

_____

_____

_____

_____

_____

_____

_____

POEM
NINETEEN

MANY SAINTS OF TODAY

God has specific guidelines on how His people are to live daily, and those guidelines can be found in His Word, the Holy Bible. Therefore, there should be no confusion about what God expects from His people, especially among those who seek His will and read His Word daily. 1 Peter 1:15-16 tells us this: "But as he which hath called you is holy, so be ye holy in all manner of conversation; Because it is written, Be ye holy; for I am holy."

MANY SAINTS OF TODAY

1979

Many saints of today are quite different from what they used to be.

We know that times are modern with all the new inventions around, but so is the saints' way of worshipping different from what I can see.

Yes, we still go to church just like saints used to do, not always because we want to but because being saints, quite naturally we are expected to.

We still sing and shout, and when the Spirit moves us, we cry, and every time we feel the need, we even testify.

Some saints always pay their tithes, and some don't even care.

Some are faithful missionaries, and some don't even have time for prayer.

Many saints take salvation for granted,
but some are trying their best to live right.

Other saints are singing and shouting on

Sunday morning and fighting on Sunday night.

Many saints think that being a Christian they will

reign with Christ the King, but being a Christian

and not living right does not profit you anything.

Yes, many saints of today are quite different from

what they used to be, because too many people

have their own theory of what a saint should be.

INS-CREATIONS NOTES:

_____

_____

_____

_____

_____

_____

_____

_____

_____

_____

_____

_____

_____

_____

_____

_____

_____

_____

_____

INS-CREATIONS NOTES:

_____

_____

_____

_____

_____

_____

_____

_____

_____

_____

_____

_____

_____

_____

_____

_____

_____

_____

_____

_____

_____

INS-CREATIONS NOTES:

_____

_____

_____

_____

_____

_____

_____

_____

_____

_____

_____

_____

_____

_____

_____

_____

_____

_____

POEM
TWENTY

TO JESUS

The Lord is my shepherd, I shall not want. He maketh me to lie down in green pastures: he leadeth me beside the still waters. He restoreth my soul: he leadeth me in the paths of righteousness for his name's sake. Yea, though I walk through the valley of the shadow of death, I will fear no evil: for thou art with me: thy rod and thy staff they comfort me. (Psalm 23:1-4)

TO JESUS
1994

Jesus, I want to always be Your friend
no matter what comes my way.

I want to have a closer relationship with
You all day, every day.

I want to understand You more as

You are directing me.

I want to submit my life to You, and Your
true friend forever be.

I will lay aside all my fears, worries, and doubts,
with my past remaining behind, as You direct
this wonderful relationship,

Yours and mine.

INS-CREATIONS NOTES:

_____

_____

_____

_____

_____

_____

_____

_____

_____

_____

_____

_____

_____

_____

_____

_____

_____

_____

_____

_____

INS-CREATIONS NOTES:

_____

_____

_____

_____

_____

_____

_____

_____

_____

_____

_____

_____

_____

_____

_____

_____

_____

_____

_____

_____

_____

POEM
TWENTY-ONE

ANOTHER YEAR

O give thanks unto the Lord: for he is good:
for his mercy endureth forever. (Psalm 136:1)

Do not take God's gift of life for granted. Every
day, show Him how grateful you are by doing
something positive for someone else, even if it is
a smile, a word of encouragement, or sharing
the message of Jesus with someone. Always live
on purpose, God's intended purpose for you.

ANOTHER YEAR

1985

Although I did nothing to deserve it, and I
cannot take the credit.
It was the goodness of the Lord so dear that
I lived to see another year.
God's grace is something I can't explain but
I thank Him for it just the same.
I will always cherish and hold it near because it
has kept me another year.
Tragedy and death have come to many,
there are few who haven't seen any,
But I lift my voice without any fear to thank the
Lord for another year.
Thank you, Jesus!

INS-CREATIONS NOTES:

_____

_____

_____

_____

_____

_____

_____

_____

_____

_____

_____

_____

_____

_____

_____

_____

_____

_____

_____

_____

INS-CREATIONS NOTES:

_____

_____

_____

_____

_____

_____

_____

_____

_____

_____

_____

_____

_____

_____

_____

_____

_____

_____

_____

POEM
TWENTY-TWO

THE LORD'S GOODNESS

Isn't it interesting that the holy scriptures often repeat themselves? For example, there are multiple verses in the Bible that encourage us to give thanks to the Lord. This gives me reason to believe that it is very important for us to remember to give thanks to the Lord regardless of what we are going through because He has been good to us all our lives. "O give thanks unto the Lord, for he is good: for his mercy endureth forever" (Psalm 107:1).

THE LORD'S GOODNESS
1984

Many days have come and gone;
another year has passed.
It is no goodness of our own that
we are here again.
It has been only by the grace of God
that we are here this very hour.
With His love He smiled on us and
brought us safely this far.
This is why we take this short time
to give all honor to the Lord,
Because if He wasn't on our side,
our lives would be of no worth.

INS-CREATIONS NOTES:

_____

_____

_____

_____

_____

_____

_____

_____

_____

_____

_____

_____

_____

_____

_____

_____

_____

_____

INS-CREATIONS NOTES:

_____

_____

_____

_____

_____

_____

_____

_____

_____

_____

_____

_____

_____

_____

_____

_____

_____

_____

_____

_____

Poem
TWENTY-THREE

STAND UP FOR JESUS

Have you ever been in a situation where you felt blocked no matter which way you turned? Have you ever felt like there were just too many obstacles in your way no matter what you tried to do? On the other hand, have you given your life to the Lord? If you have, do you believe that you can overcome any obstacle if you keep God first in your life and follow where He leads you? "Stand fast therefore in the liberty wherewith Christ has made us free and be not entangled again with the yoke of bondage" (Galatians 5:1).

STAND UP FOR JESUS
1983

Stand up for Jesus because you have
nothing to fear.
Keep your trust in Him, and He will
always be near.
As Christians, we are a city that sits high on a hill,
We must continue to do what is right
according to the Master's will.
Yes, we will have many trials, and tests
will come our way,
But if we stand up for Jesus, He will give us
directions every day.

INS-CREATIONS NOTES:

_____

_____

_____

_____

_____

_____

_____

_____

_____

_____

_____

_____

_____

_____

_____

_____

_____

_____

_____

_____

INS-CREATIONS NOTES:

_____

_____

_____

_____

_____

_____

_____

_____

_____

_____

_____

_____

_____

_____

_____

_____

_____

_____

_____

_____

_____

_____

_____

Poem
TWENTY-FOUR

SINCE I MET JESUS

If you do not have a relationship with Jesus, I encourage you to do so. Salvation is free to everybody who will accept Jesus into their heart as Lord and Savior. Acknowledge that you are a sinner, be sincerely remorseful for your sins, ask Jesus to forgive you, and to come into your life and be Lord. Get a Bible and begin to read the scriptures; ask Jesus to connect you with people who will help you on your spiritual journey.

SINCE I MET JESUS

1983

Since I met Jesus, there has been a great

change in my life!

My sins have been washed away, and I am

a new person in Christ.

He put a new song in my heart; I will lift

my voice to sing,

That Jesus is my Savior, Redeemer,

Lord, and King.

Since I met Jesus, I will patiently run this race,

And keep looking unto Jesus, the author and

finisher of my faith.

INS-CREATIONS NOTES:

_____

_____

_____

_____

_____

_____

_____

_____

_____

_____

_____

_____

_____

_____

_____

_____

_____

_____

_____

_____

_____

INS-CREATIONS NOTES:

_____

_____

_____

_____

_____

_____

_____

_____

_____

_____

_____

_____

_____

_____

_____

_____

_____

_____

_____

POEM
TWENTY-FIVE

HOLY MASTER

As a Christian, I want to live in a position where I am totally surrendered to God. I want Him to have my undivided attention, and I want to follow His will, purpose, and plans for my life. If this is going to happen for me, I must recognize God as the absolute authority in my life, and I must submit to His will regarding all aspects of my life. This means that I must allow Him to be the master of my life.

HOLY MASTER
1985

Master, you can do anything but fail.

Master, you are always willing to give me
your helping hands.

Of all the different situations I have
encountered in my life,

Master, you have never, never failed to reply.

Oh Master, I love you. Please help me
do your will.

Oh Master, I adore you. I am willing to
follow you still.

I submit myself to you as a vessel in your hands.

I will do what you want me to, Master.

I will heed your every command.

INS-CREATIONS NOTES:

_____

_____

_____

_____

_____

_____

_____

_____

_____

_____

_____

_____

_____

_____

_____

_____

_____

_____

_____

_____

_____

INS-CREATIONS NOTES:

_____
_____
_____
_____
_____
_____
_____
_____
_____
_____
_____
_____
_____
_____
_____
_____
_____
_____
_____

ABOUT THE AUTHOR

Renette Canty is an ordained minister of the Gospel and lives in Michigan. She is a Police Sergeant, having worked in the law enforcement profession for sixteen (16) years. She is a PhD candidate, has earned a Master of Philosophy in Criminal Justice, and a Master of Business Administration in Technology, and is certified in Crisis Intervention and Mental Health First Aid. Renette has a fur baby cat named Charlotte Carolina Canty, and two feather baby parakeets named Yamaha and Korg. Renette likes to sing, write poetry and songs, play her organ and keyboard, and ride her 21-speed bicycle for recreation.

If you would like to join Renette in prayer at 7:00 pm on Mondays and Thursdays, please call 712-432-3900 and enter conference ID: 394008#.

You may also send your prayer requests to Renette at charlottean4evr@yahoo.com. All communications will be kept confidential.

INS-CREATIONS

(INSPIRED CREATIONS)

Printed in the USA
CPSIA information can be obtained
at www.ICGtesting.com
CBHW051048040824
12617CB00060B/1399